Praise for *Tender Points*

"An exquisite, lyrical exploration of chronic pain, *Tender Points* is a standout."

—*The Kenyon Review*

"In *Tender Points*, Amy Berkowitz wields short form prose like a hammer, carefully but forcefully pounding away at layers of personal experience to uncover her resilient core in spite of our culture's hypocrisy about authority, power, and pain... In this short but expansive book, which reads sometimes like poetry, sometimes like philosophy, and always like resistance, Berkowitz encourages us to become authoritative about our own experiences. With necessary rage and introspection, she urges us to understand our personal, physical, and emotional pain not only as our own, but as incompletely distinct from that of culture at large."

—*Full Stop*

"*Tender Points* is a stunning work of feminist literary nonfiction about trauma and chronic pain. I read it without stopping."

—Johanna Fateman

"I was entranced and moved by Amy Berkowitz's *Tender Points*. It's a difficult book to describe (in a good way), a kind of personal detective story about trauma and the body that interrogates chronic pain literature and '90s cartoons, noise music and Anne Carson, medical listserv comment boards and video art. It's urgent, haunting, meticulously crafted, darkly comic, and it has the strangest, smartest structure of anything I've read this year. Truly unclassifiable."

—Brian Gittis, FSG's Favorite Books of 2016

"*Tender Points* is one of those books that feels necessary. It takes on rape culture and cops and doctors, the whole long history of who gets to speak and how, who gets heard and who doesn't and why not. I wish this book wasn't as necessary as it is, but I'm so grateful to Amy for writing it."

—Stephanie Young

Amy Berkowitz has written a powerful, thought-provoking, and occasionally darkly funny book on trauma and chronic pain. Would recommend to anyone who loves *Bluets*, *The Empathy Exams*, or *Heroines* by Kate Zambreno."

—Leigh Stein

"*Tender Points* is short and tough, a personal but unsentimental chronicle of trauma and chronic pain, delivered in a series of blunt, intimate fragments."

—*Longreads* (Best of 2015: Underrecognized Books)

"A movement toward regarding chronic pain, trauma, patriarchy not as the ghosts they are often painted as, but as things visceral, immediate, constant. Berkowitz writes from a place of undeniable poetics and strength."

—John Rossiter, Skylight Books, Los Angeles

"Amy Berkowitz is a poet, which lends itself seamlessly to her careful, cutting memoir about fibromyalgia, trauma and identity. In this short, lyrical work the author takes an unflinching eye toward dark moments, bringing about understanding and resilience underneath."

—*The Huffington Post*

"The fragments of *Tender Points* are a sequence of thrusts, parries, offenses, rigged by different modes and temporalities. Taken together, these fragments marshal their own negation of cohesion, linearity, the doctor's diagnostic truth. I read the venue that is *Tender Points* not as an immobile or passive point of entry, but as a dynamic, crafted instrument that blasts Berkowitz's story in high definition."

—*Entropy*

TENDER

POINTS

Originally published by Timeless, Infinite Light 2015
Printed in the United States

ISBN 978-1-64362-028-2

Designed by Joel Gregory

Nightboat Books

New York

T E N D E R
P O I N T S

Amy Berkowitz

With a new Afterword by the author

Nightboat Books

New York

I have come to believe that "revolutionary tenderness" signifies "the negation of the negation." That is, the refusal of the shittiness of our present moment and the determined insistence on optimism and in doing so, making the future life we want live in our present selves. I believe that unless we treat each other with tenderness and care now the revolution won't come. Tenderness isn't always soft, it isn't always kind or non-violent—sometimes it's a person screaming at someone else because it's the only way they can be heard—but tenderness can make things clear.

Francesca Lisette

T E N D E R

P O I N T S

▲

When I was a music journalist, I wrote that the best noise music venues are places where you walk in and think: Someone could actually die here tonight. The feeling that something real is at stake. Noise music immerses the listener in an intense and sometimes terrifying sonic experience, and without environmental cues to confirm that terror, the effect loses its power.

In "Revolutionary Letter #1," Diane di Prima writes, "I have just realized that the stakes are myself."

I'm looking for someplace dire enough to write this. I want to feel like I could actually die here tonight.

When I lived in Ann Arbor, I used to bike nine miles on an empty highway to see noise shows in Ypsilanti. The Pleasuredome was a dark unfinished basement with a concrete floor and low ceilings. Cigarettes and synths and sweat and beer. I want to write this there.

▲

Every morning I wake up feeling like I was run over by a truck. I feel like I've been hit by a bus. I wake up feeling like I got whiplash. I wake up feeling like I slept on the floor. I wake up feeling like I've been chewed up and spit out. Multiple alarms and I always feel like I've been run over by a truck.

▲

The Sphinx's riddle: What goes on four legs at dawn, two legs at noon, and three legs in the evening?

I don't particularly like riddles. But then again, neither did travelers passing through Thebes. They didn't try to solve the Sphinx's riddle because they craved the intellectual challenge. They tried to solve it because the Sphinx killed anyone who didn't.

I don't like riddles. And yet here I am, obsessed with solving a riddle of my own, the riddle of my body: Why, exactly, am I constantly in pain?

Like the Sphinx's riddle, mine is not a brainteaser. It's not Sudoku. It's not something you do on the bus to make the ride feel shorter. Like her riddle, mine has a greater urgency.

▲

In *The Culture of Pain*, David B. Morris criticizes medical literature for its tradition of approaching pain as a riddle to be answered, a challenge to be met, a puzzle to be solved. He rejects the language of conquest and asks us instead to "consider in what sense pain might be regarded not as a puzzle but as a mystery."

While a puzzle can be solved with just one or two missing pieces, pain is much more complicated, and talking about pain—especially chronic pain—as if it has an easy answer can be irresponsibly deceptive. Morris suggests that by understanding pain as a mystery, we can respect its complexity and recognize the alienating experience of living in pain. "Mysteries," he writes, "introduce us to unusual states of being... mysteries disturb the world we take for granted."

▲

An invisible illness with uncertain causes and imprecise diagnostic criteria, fibromyalgia is largely defined by its mystery.

And yet, when the onset of this pain follows a traumatic event (as it often does), it's hard not to understand that trauma as a certain kind of key. To hold that key in a palm made sweaty by too much coffee. To never put it down for the feeling that at any moment it could completely unlock the mystery and solve the problem of your pain.

▲

2 at the bottom of the neck just above the collarbone

2 just below the center of each collarbone

1 on the crease inside each elbow

2 more on the inside of each knee

On the back of the body, 2 at the bottom of the neck

1 above each shoulder blade and just inside each shoulder blade

2 on either side of the lower spine

2 more on the outer part of each hamstring

In order to be diagnosed, the patient must experience discomfort in at least 11 of 18 tender points designated by the American College of Rheumatology.

▲

I agree that pain is something more complex and un-knowable than a puzzle. And yet, when it comes to the mystery of my pain, I can't resist the impulse to solve it. I have all these pieces, and I can't stop my hands from wanting to jam them together until some sense emerges.

When I think about my clues, they are inside a wicker basket that I'm carrying through the woods. It's night-time. It's quiet. I realize that, for some reason, I am Little Red Riding Hood. Why? I should be thinking of Nancy Drew or Harriet the Spy. Some story about a girl detective, not about a girl waylaid in the woods.

But to solve this kind of mystery, it seems, you need to walk alone into a forest. You need to walk until you meet a wolf.

Throughout pop culture, Little Red Riding Hood's wolf is read as a sexual predator, from Sam the Sham's se-ductive canine to Susan Brownmiller's rapist.

I have a wolf in my story. But he will not interrupt my walk through the forest. Which is to say he's already interrupted it: He's the reason I'm here, sorting out the aftermath. Which is to say the wolf is eternally interrupting my walk through the forest: emerging from behind the same tree again and again to block my path. Imagine it repeating like a GIF.

My Little Red Riding Hood has no granny in the woods. She has no treats in her basket. Her basket is for gathering clues. A handful of fur or a whisker she yanks from his face. Could be DNA tested later.

▲

"Acutely traumatized people... are generally dominated by the sympathetic fight/flight system. They tend to suffer from flashbacks and racing hearts."

Peter Levine, *In an Unspoken Voice*

▲

In 1989, Kathleen Hanna traveled to Seattle to take a writing workshop with Kathy Acker. Acker asked Hanna why she wanted to write, and Hanna said: "Because nobody has ever listened to me in my whole life, and I have all this stuff that I want to say."

Acker replied: "Then why are you doing spoken word? You should be in a band. Because nobody goes to spoken word, but people go to see bands."

We know how the story ends: Hanna goes home and starts Bikini Kill, the legendary punk band largely responsible for pioneering the riot grrrl movement and changing the face of feminism.

▲

When you have all this stuff that you want to say, how do you get people to listen?

There are thousands of blog posts about how to write compelling blog posts. Many of these posts discuss the practical benefits of writing listicles, or articles in the form of lists.

9 Reasons to Use a Content Management System

17 Power Snacks for Studying

33 Shiba Inu Puppies Who Just Can't Contain Themselves Right Now

Listicles are a powerful way to drive traffic to your blog. People love listicles: They're fun to read and they're highly shareable via social media. The content is easy to digest and the authoritative headlines command respect.

4 Events You Miss Because of Fibromyalgia Pain

1. **Brunch with Marissa's Parents**

Your alarm goes off at 9:30, then 9:45. Marissa's parents are in town and brunch is at 11. The alarm goes off again at 10. 10:05. You feel like you've been hit by a truck, which is how you feel every morning. 10:15. If you don't shower, you can still get there almost on time. 10:25. 10:40. Fuck. You can make it if you call a cab. It would be like $20. Everything hurts. It's like you're under a brick the size of your body. Okay, it's 10:55. You text Marissa that you feel sick, that you're so sorry, tell your parents I say hi.

2. **Company Outing to the Roller Rink**

Last time you went roller-skating, the heavy rental skates misaligned your anklebones and your physical therapist shook her head as she popped them back in. Nobody believes you when you say you would love to go. Least of all your boss, who already worries that you're not a team player. But you really would love to go: You, too were once a little kid who thrilled at swooping around rinks to *Groove Is in the Heart* and *Turn the Beat Around*. It's just that's not your reality now. But the tyranny of mandatory fun is bearing down. Everyone's eyes are on your ankles, and they won't be satisfied until they see scars or bandages or blood.

3. The Noise Show at Lobot Gallery

You forget their name, but it's Alexandra's roommate's band, and they're supposed to be really good. You told Alexandra you'd go. You told Alexandra's roommate you'd go. But you are not gonna go. Last time you saw a show there, your muscles tensed up in the cold warehouse and standing on the concrete floor for three hours made your bones ache. Standing still is somehow harder than moving, and confronted with the shimmering drone of the headliner, your body froze and felt like it could chip as easily as ice.

4. Yoga with Carrie

Yoga helps, but only when you go regularly. Every time you go to yoga after taking a break for a while, one 60-minute class can make you feel sick for days. If you go to yoga with Carrie tonight, it's likely you'll feel like shit the rest of the week. Which would be bad because you're meeting with a client tomorrow. Late to work and home straight after. Pain lost in your muscles, trying to find a way out, slams you down in bed but won't let you sleep.

▲

It's worth noting that it's particularly difficult for a woman's voice to command respect. To quote Kathleen Hanna again: "There's this certain assumption that when a man tells the truth, it's the truth. And when, as a woman, I go to tell the truth, I feel like I have to negotiate the way I'll be perceived... There's always the suspicion around a woman's truth—the idea that you're exaggerating."

▲

Poetry fails me because it's not written plainly. Its oblique nature aligns too closely with the slippery and unreliable speech that women have been associated with since ancient Greece.

In "The Gender of Sound," Anne Carson writes, "Woman as a species is frequently said to lack the ordering principle of sophrosyne." Sophrosyne is a masculine virtue: the use of moderation and self-control in speaking.

While men speak with order, Carson observes that "the women of classical literature are a species given to disorderly and uncontrolled outflow of sound—to shrieking, wailing, sobbing, shrill lament, loud laughter, screams of pain or pleasure, and eruptions of raw emotion in general."

▲

That's why I so firmly want prose here. Sentences. Periods. Male certainty. These are facts. No female vocal fry. No uptalk. No question about what I tell you. No metaphor. Go ahead. Fact check. "Did I stutter." Fuck off.

I'm writing about the violence of patriarchal culture. I'm writing about the uneven balance of power in female-patient/male-doctor relationships. I'm aware of a certain home-team advantage, and I will not dare write this in anything that can't pass for straight masculine prose. It's not that this isn't *écriture féminine,* but it's *écriture féminine en homme.*

▲

While chronic pain is hardly a puzzle with an easy answer, it can be equally damaging to insist on its mysteriousness—particularly in the case of fibromyalgia pain.

Fibromyalgia is routinely described in terms of its lack of certainty or credibility. Even the National Institute of Health has a troublingly vague grasp of the illness; its website explains that "the causes of fibromyalgia are unknown, but there are probably a number of factors involved."

Up to 90 percent of fibromyalgia patients are female, and there is a strong precedent for "women's voices not being heard or considered credible in the male-dominated healthcare system," as noted in "The Girl Who Cried Pain," a study by Diane E. Hoffman and Anita J. Tarzian. While I can't say for certain how fibromyalgia would be discussed if the condition primarily affected men, I suspect that we would see words like "mysterious" and "unknown" drop from the literature, replaced by the findings—however incomplete—of research done thus far.

▲

"Drug Approved. Is Disease Real?"

This was the title of a *New York Times* article about fibromyalgia published the year I was diagnosed.

▲

Riding my bike to the doctor's office in Fort Greene, I am aware of vibrations from the handlebars and how they make my wrists and hands tingle and go numb. The usual shoulder pain and a weakness in my hips but I can ride my bike. It's a mild winter day in 2008 and I'm wearing a silk scarf around my neck to keep the wind off my skin.

I lock my bike outside and walk into the small office. The doctor asks about my pain. He presses my body in 18 places. My back, my shoulders, legs, arms, neck. Where does it hurt. He walks into another room, I'll be right back. I hear a printer hum. He comes back with a sheet of paper: a diagram of a body with 18 tender points. A diagnosis of fibromyalgia.

Fine with me. A great relief to have a name for this. I know the true name of this disease—My Body Is Haunted by a Certain Trauma—so I don't much care what other name it has, so long as it has one. Something to point to. Something to call it.

And later, yes, I get the blood work done. No Lyme, no lupus, no whatever else. Confirms the sloppy diagnosis of exclusion. Fine with me.

▲

The answer to the Sphinx's riddle, by the way, is a person: Four legs when they crawl as a baby, two legs when they walk, and three in old age when they use a cane.

Though I currently walk on two legs, I have a friend who is also diagnosed with fibromyalgia who uses a wheelchair. I'm not sure how many legs the Sphinx would count that as.

The tremendous difference between my friend's symptoms and mine make me think of the suspicion that exists around the fibromyalgia diagnosis. While I do believe the diagnosis is useful—at least in the limited sense that there is value in giving a name to something with no name and thereby giving it legitimacy—it's only a starting point.

▲

Perhaps because of her dual identity as a physician who specializes in treating fibromyalgia and a fibromyalgia patient, Dr. Ginevra Liptan has an unusually nuanced understanding of the illness. Based on a synthesis of medical studies and her own clinical research, Liptan's explanation is unencumbered by the uncertainties that impede most others.

In *Figuring Out Fibromyalgia*, she writes, "Ultimately, all the symptoms of fibromyalgia stem from abnormal activation of the fight-or-flight nervous system."

A chain reaction follows:

"Deep sleep is inhibited because the brain is trying to stay alert to fend off danger. A lack of deep sleep causes fatigue and prevents adequate growth hormone release. A lack of growth hormone interferes with the normal muscle tissue repair process and leads to muscle pain. Muscles and their surrounding connective tissue are chronically tightened to respond to danger and become painful. The pain signals streaming up to the brain from muscles overwhelm the nervous system and cause it to become hyper-reactive to pain."

▲

"Illness is the only form of 'life' possible under capitalism."

The Socialist Patients' Collective

In 1970, a German activist group called the Socialist Patients' Collective recognized capitalism as the root cause of all illness. To be sick, then, was a political act: a passive resistance against capitalism. The group's slogan: "Turn illness into a weapon."

▲

A few years after I graduated college with a degree in literature, I found myself working at the world's largest market research company. My job was analyzing consumer sentiment as expressed in online spaces. This was another way of saying that I spent eight hours a day lurking on message boards.

The company's biggest clients were pharmaceutical companies, which meant that the message boards I lurked on were message boards for people with cancer and other serious illnesses.

As you would expect, these messages, written by sick people and their caregivers, were intensely emotional.

I am so happy the scans were good! Healing hugs and blessings. <<<hugs>>> Hugs to you and yours. Love and hugs. Prayers and hugs. Take good care everyone! My prayers are with you. Keep us posted.

But the world's largest market research company was uninterested in emotion. What they had me looking for was sentiment: I scored each sample as Positive, Negative, Neutral, Unsure, or No Opinion. People and their details were shucked away, unless they were significant enough to be included in the qualitative results.

My job was to leverage this data to identify key factors that would make sick and dying people more interested in purchasing very expensive medicine.

DH is on erbitux/oxaliplatin/5fu/leucovorin. He has the erbitux rash BAD, but onco is hesitant to prescribe an antibiotic.

It was while I was immersed in this culture of online illness, with its own language of acronyms and emoticons, that I got sick myself.

▲

Working hurt. The precise mousing of data entry made my wrists tingle and go numb, and sitting at the keyboard made my shoulder muscles spasm. On the worst days, the stiffness spread to my hips and legs. The doctor in Fort Greene wrote a letter recommending a two-week rest period.

I faxed his letter to the HR department of the world's largest market research company. I called and emailed and they didn't answer. I left messages that they didn't return. I applied for short-term disability, and my claim was rejected twice.

When the two weeks were over, I didn't feel any better. The doctor recommended another week of rest. I faxed, emailed, called HR. I was met with the same radio silence, which was starting to sound an awful lot like a static crackle softly whispering *you lazy cunt we don't believe you're sick, trying to trick us you worthless piece of shit.*

Coincidentally, I came back to work the same day as another analyst who had been out sick. He had broken his ankle snowboarding, and he was wearing a boot. His cubicle was decorated with get well soon cards, and an Edible Arrangement bloomed festive pineapple chunks next to his monitor.

My cube was as bare as I'd left it. A get well soon card would have acknowledged the fact of my illness, and as far as the world's largest market research company was concerned, I was faking it.

Picturing my cubicle next to my coworker's is a perfect illustration of Morris's differentiation between male and female pain.

In *The Culture of Pain*, he writes: "Female pain is regularly disregarded, discounted, and dismissed, largely because it does not always conform to the clear organic model of appendicitis or a broken arm."

▲

As I read more about the history of invisible illness, I'm surprised and amused to diagnose myself with hysteria.

▲

They're just nasty fat women who want to collect disability checks. "Doing stuff makes me tired, give me some money and/or drugs." Lazy-ass slugs who sit at home and watch Judge Judy *while the rest of the world works for a living. 71% of them are fat women who don't ever get off their ass. Sorry if you don't like facts.*

Anyone who can read an Internet article and say "ow" 11 times can have it.

▲

In *The Body in Pain,* Elaine Scarry describes pain's essential inexpressibility: "For the person in pain, so incontestably and unnegotiably present is it, that 'having pain' may come to be thought of as the most vibrant example of what it is to 'have certainty,' while for the other person it is so elusive that 'hearing about pain' may exist as the primary model of what it is 'to have doubt.'"

▲

Fibromyalgia is largely defined by a lack of visible symptoms or identifying lab tests. The only diagnostic criteria are the frustratingly vague tender points. Press here and I'll tell you if it hurts. Now press here. Now press here.

All I have to do is tell you. All you have to do is believe what I tell you.

▲

I have to deal with these nutcases at work and I flat out call them fakers to their face. They need to get up off their lard-asses and get a job. They're just whiney people who love to be "sick."

I knew a woman with it; she was miserable and had a whole Myspace dedicated to the constant pain.

▲

At the Vital Forms symposium in 2013, Melissa Buzzeo asked questions:

"Why people who are sick are also looked at as waste products in society. Why people, especially women, especially sick women, do not want to draw too much attention to themselves... What does it mean to talk about yourself."

Welcome to the Myspace of my constant pain.

▲

I'm 21 years old and I feel like I'm 50. I'm 50, I feel like I'm 90. I am only 22 and I feel like I am like 60 or 70 years old. I feel like I'm in my 80s, but I'm only 46.

People in my life may think I am exaggerating but I am truly in pain.

▲

I sent some of this writing to a friend who also writes about pain. She sent me an email about my writing, and her writing, and she added, "Also, on a side slash main note, I'm sorry to hear you are living with chronic pain. It sucks in every way."

I don't remember how it feels not to be in pain. At the doctor's office, pain scales are impossible because I lost my zero. I choose a number because I'm supposed to choose a number.

It's only when the pain is severe or when the pain prevents me from doing something that I'm forced to think about it. But even when I'm not thinking about it, it's still there. My body is riding BART and it's in pain. My body is peeling an orange and it's in pain. My body is worrying about something stupid and it's in pain. My body is writing this and it's in pain.

What I'm trying to say is: I like what my friend wrote. Chronic pain is always on a side slash main note.

▲

The story of my pain is not an easy story to tell. And I'm not talking about the emotional difficulty of telling it; I mean the plot itself is confusing. Trauma is nonlinear. There are flashbacks and flash-forwards. And my story is a story about forgetting. Forgetting is one of the main characters; in fact, he may be the hero. Forgetting swoops down on a rope to rescue me right after my rape. He holds me with his free arm as we swing back to safety, saying, "You can't handle this right now, but you'll remember when you're 23, and you'll have better psychological defenses then, and a good therapist."

If Forgetting is the hero of the story, who is Memory? And what happens to Memory in the end?

▲

There's a *This American Life* segment about a couple that's furnishing their new apartment. They buy a table on eBay at a very reasonable price. When it arrives, they realize they've accidentally ordered dollhouse furniture. The table is two-and-a-half inches, not two-and-a-half feet tall. Smaller than most of the things they were planning to put on it.

This dollhouse table feels familiar.

My memory of that day is in miniature. Although it's very clear, it's about two-and-a-half inches tall and stuck inside my head. I can't show it to anybody. I can't locate a corresponding full-size memory out in the world. And I can't even tell you what day *that day* was.

▲

In 2012, somebody decided to figure out exactly which day the song "It Was a Good Day" was written about.

By analyzing Ice Cube's lyrics, Donovan Strain ultimately concluded that the only day when *Yo! MTV Raps* was on the air, the weather was clear and smogless in LA, beepers were commercially available, and the Lakers beat the SuperSonics was January 20, 1992.

I worry that I'm starting to fetishize this project of resurrecting the past.

▲

I keep having this vision of my body shot through with systems of hidden stairs and hallways—secret, steep, ill-maintained servants' quarters. Imagine that the stairs climb up my arm and neck and lead to doors in and out my ears, then back down the other arm. In these dim, drafty passages, memories creep through my body right next to present perceptions.

After the death of her husband, Sarah Winchester used her share of the Winchester rifle fortune to build a sprawling and peculiar mansion to appease the spirits of the vast number of people killed by her husband's rifles. Convinced that the spirits would murder her if she ever stopped construction, Sarah hired workers to build round the clock, so that the house was never complete. This continued for 36 years, until her death in 1922.

Most people with fibromyalgia experience non-restorative sleep; that is, no matter how long they sleep, they wake up feeling tired. Like many things about fibromyalgia, the cause of this sleep disorder is unknown, but many doctors believe that the problem starts with a constant activation of the sympathetic nervous system's fight-or-flight response, which increases nocturnal vigilance and prevents restful sleep.

What vigil is my sympathetic nervous system keeping? It seems to be supervising construction of a mansion designed to ward off evil spirits. It's building secret passages inside my body to route the past around the present and keep trauma out of sight, like servants in a smoothly running household.

▲

The act

and the words

that excused it:

You're older now   so I have to do this

▲

Why were we alone in the exam room?
That's the question that trips everything up
The hole in the story (the story is a hole)

Why were we alone in the exam room?
My mother went to speak with the billing office
Or the nurse left to check on another room
Or the nurse was right there but didn't see
Or refused to see

Or maybe you had to be up close to notice
The particular way my doctor's hand was moving
The dumb wild grabbing
The imprecise thrusting

I looked in his eyes as he raped me
He saw my look and my look said:
There is no fucking way this is part of the exam
Stared up at him like that until he was done

▲

FTP

Doctors are cops

Self-select into the profession like a disease

That will never be diagnosed

Because its name is health

And its smell is soap

Walk around swinging their clubs

Talking too loud

Killing people all the time

(It's their job so it's fine)

And who can argue with a stethoscope

▲

Why were we alone in the exam room?
That's the question that trips everything up
The hole in the story
That makes people doubt me
Or does it just make me doubt

Well fuck the doubt
I mean fuck it dead

It happened as it happened
In my head

10 years old

Men don't doubt
So why should I

I've just discovered my opinions are facts
Same as any man with a dick to wag around

▲

The problem is
You can't put pain on trial

▲

Ashley Brim 1/10/15 1:36 PM

Comment: *I read that the haunted Winchester House is a myth. That Sarah actually just had a lot of money, was an architect, and liked her workers, who would be out of a job if she stopped building. With her continuous projects, they just lived with their families on the grounds and around the house. She was very brilliant, ran her own company, and had many inventions. This image of her as a crazy woman was just patriarchy condemning her because she never remarried and lived her life like a man, traveling and running a company.*

But don't change this. This fits well here. And there is no right story.

▲

I've been thinking a lot about Krang lately.

Krang is one of the villains from *Teenage Mutant Ninja Turtles*. He's a brain without a body who uses an "exo-suit" or "robot body" for mobility. He used to have a body, but for reasons that are never explained, he lost it when he was banished from Dimension X. This happened before the start of the show, so we never see what Krang looked like before he was banished.

Krang is angry. That "ang" is half his name. Other villains are angry, too, but their anger is a cold, sweeping, wrathful anger. Krang's anger is more personal, petty. He's cranky—that's the other half of his name. His voice is a high-pitched feminine whine that sounds like a mean caricature of a mother-in-law.

A lot of the time, he's angry about his disability. He moans, "My robot body is not working!" and "There would be no problem if I had a body!"

I googled "Krang" and "disability" and all of the results were videos of *Teenage Mutant Ninja Turtles* episodes with comments disabled or embedding disabled.

▲

I'm hanging out with a friend who just finished her MFA, and she's telling me about her job search. She shrugs and says, "Well, I can always go back to being a barista for a while."

I am bitterly jealous of people who can always go back to being a barista for a while.

▲

It's 2010 and my boyfriend's bed is like a Reese's Peanut Butter Cup. Brown comforter and pillow and tan sheets the exact color of peanut butter. He makes me omelets with expensive ingredients and buys me a record player for my birthday. This, I think, is care.

I'm having a hard time finding a job because I just moved to the city and because my disability substantially narrows my options. Avoid repetitive motions. That's kind of the definition of a job, repetitive motions.

The temp agency called it administrative *slash* data entry, but it turns out to be pure data entry. I'm entering data from massive binders of handwritten medical records into a series of online forms. The data is so thick with abbreviations that I have no idea what any of it means.

It's a terrible office, with low, square-tiled ceilings; everything beige and dusty. I sit in a cubicle on a mostly deserted floor. I scavenge the empty cubes for thick reference books and a cardboard box so I can make a monitor riser and a footrest and approximate an ergonomic setup.

Despite these interventions, I can't physically tolerate the work. By my fourth week, my wrist feels tight and numb as it hovers above the ten-key. I try wearing a brace, but it doesn't help. I tell my supervisor, and within the hour, I get a call from the temp agency informing me that the assignment is over.

That night, I can't stop crying. I'm angry at my body, I'm angry at the temp agency, I'm angry at the man I blame for this pain. And I'm overwhelmed thinking: How the fuck am I ever going to support myself.

And my boyfriend says, "Well, don't wallow in it. That's not going to help. Just pick yourself up and get back out there."

These are the words of a little league coach but I am not a little league team. I am a grown person with a disability.

After that, his bed doesn't look like a giant piece of chocolate anymore. It looks like a bed.

▲

Ten years after the rape
But before I remembered the rape
And before the pain diffused throughout my body
It was localized in one place: You can guess where

The condition was called vulvodynia
It's exactly what it sounds like:
Vulvo—vulva, dynia—pain

I should rewatch that *Sex and the City* episode where
Charlotte has it. What narrative do they give it?

Episode 50:

Charlotte's Doctor: It's not serious. It's mostly just
uncomfortable. We can get it under control.

Carrie: Your vagina's depressed?!

Carrie and Miranda make jokes.

Charlotte: You guys, stop! I might have vulvodynia.

Carrie: Vulvo*whati*a?

Carrie and Miranda make jokes.

Fortunately for Charlotte, her doctor is apparently right.
It's not serious. In fact, the pain disappears so quickly,
it's gone by episode 51.

This misrepresentation pissed off a lot of people, including Vulvodynia Association Director Phyllis Mate, who observed that the show "failed miserably at portraying the serious and complicated nature of this condition."

Episode 51:

Carrie is drawn to jazz musician Ray King, who flirts with her and gets her number. Mr. Big is noticeably annoyed.

▲

Winter 2005: I felt so alone in this pain. I found a LiveJournal group called vvs-community and that group saved my life. I wanted to find something more original and accurate to say than "saved my life," but that's pretty much what it did.

Through the group, I was introduced to a woman who was doing a survey about vulvodynia for her PhD thesis. I met her at a dive bar on St. Marks Place, and she interviewed me there, in the little nook by the window. All of the questions were easy to answer except one. Do you have a partner? Yes. Do you have pain with sex? Yes. Do you experience pain constantly? Yes. Do you use birth control pills? No. Have you ever been raped or sexually abused?

I... don't... know.

I was shocked by my answer. I thought I knew. I thought I knew I hadn't. But no one had ever asked me that, and the question was an invitation to feel something I had been trying not to feel for a very long time.

▲

I was so alone. There was the vvs-community group, but I didn't know anyone else who had it, not in real life. And it's not the kind of thing you talk about.

My boyfriend was in Germany, which was good, because it absolved me of any opportunity to fail at having sex with him.

My boyfriend was in Germany, which was bad, because he was in Germany and I was in Brooklyn.

My window looked out on Bushwick Avenue, which is a major truck route. Soot collected on the windowsill and the air was always gray or maybe I was imagining that. That's where I would sit when I called him, in a chair by the window.

I bought so many phone cards that year. I bought them online, so there's no actual card; you just buy a really long number. I went through them so fast that I never memorized them. I scribbled them in the back of whatever book I was reading. These numbers were the magic spells that transported my boyfriend's voice to Brooklyn.

I would just call him and cry. I remember one day it was raining and the window and the sky were both streaky and gray. Already crying, I dialed one of those long numbers, and my boyfriend picked up and I cried.

I don't think I had anything to say—or I did, but the only way to say it was crying. If I said anything it was, "I'm so sorry I'm crying. I just can't stop crying. I'm so sorry."

My boyfriend was at school, in between classes. He was sitting on a hill under a tree, which was the only place he could get reception on campus. I know that I cried for more than an hour, and finally my tremendously patient boyfriend said he had to go; his class was starting and the sun was setting and it was getting very cold up on the hill under the tree.

OVERSLEPT / SO TIRED / IF LATE / GET FIRED /
WHY BOTHER / WHY THE PAIN / JUST GO HOME /
DO IT AGAIN

This poem, line by line, was printed across great beams above my head as I rushed along with throngs of other miserable people, every single morning Monday through Friday, trudging under the lines about "IF LATE / GET FIRED" at 8:50, let's be real, 8:55 a.m. Midtown Manhattan is a kind of hell, and I was living in a handful of other hells, too.

One hell was my boss, who was peculiarly cruel. My first day, she said she wouldn't train me, her previous assistant would, which sounded fine until her previous assistant came over and gave me a look and said, "I have no idea why she wants me to train you—she said I did everything wrong." And so I repeated the mistakes I was taught how to make, and my boss never lacked a reason to criticize or blame me.

But the main hell was the pain: Since I moved home to New York after college, my vagina had been hurting for no discernable reason. The pain was compounded by the crisp crotches of the Ann Taylor Loft pants I bought for that awful job. This and my boyfriend was away in Germany for a year.

And every morning, getting off at 42nd Street Times Square, those words were a very blunt way of taking

stock of my life: "WHY BOTHER / WHY THE PAIN."
On at least one occasion, I very nearly let the "JUST
GO HOME" convince me to turn around and head back
to Brooklyn.

Every morning, I marveled at the city's decision to
put such a depressing poem in a place where so many
people would see it every day. Finally I stopped looking
at it. I took a different exit that was out of my way and
made me later but I didn't care.

Why the pain.

I did most of my life's crying that year. I cried through
Midtown after gynecologist appointments, and I cried
in South Park Slope after appointments with the acu-
puncturist who so strangely had the same name as the
doctor who raped me. (Though I didn't remember the
rape until two years after the acupuncture, so at the
time, I just thought of him as my pediatrician.)

So what did I do. I read the vvs-community LiveJournal.
I learned to wear skirts with sweater tights instead of
pants. I took antidepressants. I asked friends at work
for advice about my boss. They said to leave a blazer
at my desk and always wear it when I go into her office
so that she would respect me more, and the idea that
a blazer could, should matter that much made me too
angry to do it.

▲

In *Close to the Knives*, David Wojnarowicz describes taking a sick friend to Long Island to see a doctor who's developed a controversial treatment for AIDS.

I haven't read it in years, but the details stick in my mind: the sick friend bundled in blankets in the back seat, the fake wood paneling in the doctor's office, the depressing vista of used car lots they pass on the way home.

The persistence of these details, details that are not mine, casts a harsh light on the blanks in my own memory. What do I remember about my own doctors' visits?

▲

Through message board rumors, I'd hear about vulvodynia specialists with hopeful-sounding cures. All of these doctors were men. I'd travel around the city to their offices and walk out feeling variously disappointed, disrespected, depressed, and angry.

Because my boyfriend lived in Germany, I almost always went to these appointments alone. One time, though, he came with me. I can't tell you what neighborhood the office was in. I can't tell you what train we took.

I would like to tell the whole story. I don't want to make things up. I would like to tell it how it happened, and that I can't do this feels frustrating.

I remember a TV in the waiting room. I remember I went in to speak with the doctor and he got straight to the point: Surgery is your only option. Cut out the nerves that feel the pain. Simple.

I walked out and met my boyfriend and I don't remember if I started crying in the waiting room or once we'd walked outside, but once I started crying I did not stop. It must have been cold because I remember we went into a Barnes & Noble to keep warm until I stopped crying.

I have fragments. I remember it was cold. I remember more or less what the doctor said. I remember the waiting room had a TV. But I don't have the complete narrative.

And so the black holes in my memory become part of the story. I mean, they are the story.

▲

Actually this is surprisingly concise:

Start when I'm 24
Then flash back   /   literally

To age 10   /   'or so'
I can never pin down exactly when
To the rape
That it took me five years to call rape
And then flash back again
To age 21
When my vagina started to hurt
For no reason   /   'for no reason'
And the carousel of white male doctors
Started to spin

They had opinions   /   lacked compassion
Saw my vagina like a fish
Flopping on land
Something
Very clearly outside myself
And very clearly doomed
Their opinions were facts
Because they were white male doctors
And I walked around soaked in tears
For a little more than a year
Until the symptoms started to subside
And now, age 29   /   30 by the time I edit this
I step back inside that soggy year

And I recognize the face of my rapist
On every one of those doctors
Realize I spent 2005 reenacting my rape
Without knowing it

1993 raped   /   without knowing the word rape
So it was filed in a stack of other memories
And fastened there with shame
Rape faded like a normal memory   /   only not:
2007 it came back in a sick vision
That looked too bright and real
Like a photo illustration on a cake
Saw the doctor
Saw the room
Saw the window
Next morning woke up in pain

▲

Why black box recorders often fail:

The voice recorder only captures the final two hours
The battery life is short
The signal range is only a few miles
It is a small object to find
It doesn't float

▲

Here's a doctor I remember:
A hero on the message boards
A six-month wait to see him
Weill Cornell Medical Center
Vulvodynia specialist blah blah blah

And when I saw him, I took off my clothes
And he looked at my skin
He had a theory
About pigmentation
And vulvar pain
And I was so much a piece of meat
He scratched my stomach
To see the mark it would leave
(This was part of the study)
And he said to me, "You have porcelain skin"
I wanted to hit him

I asked him about the side effects
Of the drug he wanted me to try
Exasperated, my good doctor said
"You can't believe
Everything you read
On the Internet"

▲

Browsing the American College of Rheumatology website's page on fibromyalgia, I'm drawn to a section called POINTS TO REMEMBER. The first bullet point reads: "Look forward, not backward. Focus on what you need to do to get better, not what caused your illness."

Maybe this is good advice. I don't know, because I've done the opposite. Looking forward does not satisfy me; before I treat the symptoms, I want to investigate the tangled chain of events that got me here. Looking backward is what I need to do to get better.

▲

Last year, I went to PS1 with my friend Marissa to see the Mike Kelley show.

An accident had recently happened at the museum: A guest had stumbled and knocked over a sculptural installation. So there were loads of security guards patrolling the exhibit, and they became part of the art. Kelley's videos already evoke an uncomfortable voyeuristic feeling, so having a uniformed guard tell you ma'am, please step back from the screen almost felt like being caught masturbating.

I was intent on watching the video of the boy at the barbershop all the way through—how the barber wore a white coat like a doctor's coat—but Marissa came to get me and said you should really check out the next room for the thing you're writing.

The piece she wanted to show me was *Horizontal Tracking Shot of a Cross Section of Trauma Rooms*: Behind a row of painted panels, three screens showed sliding blocks of solid colors accompanied by a ticking soundtrack, which were interrupted by very short clips of children experiencing traumas—crying, being tormented, etc.

I sat on the bench and watched the cycle a couple of times. Kelley's footage is sourced from home movies on

YouTube, and looks like the sort of thing you might see on *America's Funniest Home Videos*. The people who sat down next to me laughed at the clips the way you're supposed to laugh at *America's Funniest Home Videos*.

Their laughter surprised me, because my reaction to the piece was so different: I saw it as a realistic representation of how trauma functions. The way the short video clips are embedded into a neutral background is an elegant illustration of the way shards of trauma bury themselves in our minds.

6 Essential Items for Your Post-Traumatic Stress
Disorder Cave

1. Unemployed Boyfriend

With few commitments, your unemployed boyfriend
has plenty of time to spend hanging out in your cave.
No job means no need to shave, so it's likely that he
has a sexy beard. Because he's depressed, a cave
feels comfortable to him, too. Like you, he's grateful
for its shelter. Although talking about emotions may
not come naturally to him, he has felt terrible pain,
and he is kind.

2. Pot

Have you ever wanted the world to stop existing? Pot
kind of works for that. While the world may contain
rapists, twice-denied short-term disability claims, and
any number of other revolting and evil things, the cave
contains nothing revolting or evil. Seal the barrier
between cave and world with a thick plume of smoke.

3. Power Pop

In the late 1970s, thousands of men in denim jack-
ets were hard at work writing the tightest, catchiest
three-minute pop songs about love and girls and nice
weather. While most of these songs have been forgot-
ten, so many of them achieve perfection. Only people

who have known real pain can make songs so precisely engineered to manifest feelings of dumb, broad joy. *Shake Some Action, Live in the Sun, Blast the Pop, No Matter What, Rave It Up, Tomorrow Belongs to You.* Invite the songs into your cave.

4. Condoms

Your unemployed boyfriend is gorgeous, and fucking him is the opposite of everything bad. You fuck while you're having conversations. You fuck while you're eating clementines. You fuck while you're listening to power pop comps. You point out the drum fills to him. You lick his ear and stop to say, This part's really good.

5. Flashbacks

It wouldn't be a post-traumatic stress disorder cave without flashbacks to the trauma that made you retreat. The trauma was rape, so the flashbacks happen during sex. When you start to dissociate, stop and tell your boyfriend you feel scared. Ask him to please tell you his name and where you are. What year it is and how old you are. To please just keep telling you things about where you are. He holds you until you understand you're 24 and he's your boyfriend and you're in your messy cave room in Brooklyn.

6. Diner

Getting out of the cave gets you out of your head; getting into the world gets you out of the memories that try to trap you. It feels good to put on clothes and walk to the diner. The diner is called Cozy Corner or it's called Jimmy's or it's called Delight Diner and Donuts. You don't know it, but you're hungry and you're probably dehydrated. Get a grilled cheese and a Coke and watch something on TV. Now you're ready to return to your cave.

▲

"My pain vanishes in the molecular attention to your vibrating life. Let's make the world anew."

Petra Kuppers

When I looked in your eyes, I didn't feel any pain. When I touched you. So I spent as much time with you as possible.

Everything else was painful: The literal pain, the job that made it worse, the flashbacks to the trauma that caused it. Sometimes I'd drape an icepack on my shoulder or my wrist. But being with you was the only thing that really helped.

I rang the doorbell, and you came downstairs in your boxers and a dirty black T-shirt.

You didn't leave the house much. You'd quit your job because you hated it, and now you stayed up late every night learning things on Wikipedia, smoking pot and listening to records, slept all day. At night you'd go to the bar, or haul your gear to Goodbye Blue Monday to play a noise set with Matt. But during the day, you mostly stayed indoors. You'd meet me downstairs in your boxers and your dirty black T-shirt and you'd say hey.

Your deep sadness resonated with my deep sadness and I decided I would make you feel better. I would help you revise your resume and find a sliding-scale therapist.

I called you until you answered the phone. Can I come over. I wrapped some cookies in tinfoil and put on a red dress. I biked through five neighborhoods in the dark. At your house I would take off the dress, unwrap the tinfoil. I wanted to be some bright thing in your dim life. I was a flower, waiting to bloom for you. It sounds stupid, but that's what I was.

▲

Looking at an old photo of you performing—one hand on the mixer and one hand holding a bottle of Ancient Age—I'm reminded of how much the drinking was part of the playing. There wasn't much to do in that particular set-up—just the mixer and a couple of pedals. So it was all theatrics. And one way to act is the act of obliterating yourself so you can melt down and live inside the big, awful sound you're making.

In this way, noise is the music of the teenage boy who opens his mouth to say how he feels and then realizes he doesn't know how he feels or how to talk about it even if he did.

And I don't mean to say that noise music is inarticulate. Not at all. I only mean that noise music is a gorgeous metaphor for a certain communication breakdown.

As bell hooks writes in *The Will to Change: Men, Masculinity, and Love*, young men raised in our culture "know the rules." That is, "they know they must not express feelings, with the exception of anger." And when you look at some of the best and most sincere music the men I care about were making when we were coming of age ten years ago: It was noise.

We're destroying ourselves so that you won't look at us / We'll be too drunk to remember this / Don't look at us, okay? Just listen

▲

After you played a set at that Polish bar in Greenpoint that let us have noise shows until the regular clientele complained, and after I helped you carry the gear up-stairs, you wanted to listen to the recording. Seriously? I'd just heard it. Whatever, okay.

You put it on and it sounded completely different. I could hear nuances in the music that had been com-pletely obscured by the deafening volume at the bar.

"This is really good," I said. "Why don't you play less loud so people can actually hear it?"

"Matt wants it loud. He always wants to play as loud as possible. That's his thing."

This is the horrible sound we make and you can't leave / Our big noise is shaking you but you can't hear what's inside / We'll be too drunk to remember this / Don't listen to us, okay? Just hear how loud we are

▲

One night at the Pleasuredome, I arrived to find the bands set up in Jono's bedroom instead of the basement. In Jono's doorway, a sweaty noise musician stood in front of a theremin with one hand over the wire and the other holding a can of beer. Eyes closed, he played the instrument with his whole body, swaying into it and changing its moan. He rested his beer on top of the theremin, lowering the pitch, and absentmindedly opened another can. His sweaty, eyes-shut performance continued, unsteady on his feet, playing inebriation as an instrument. I thought there was real humor in this— one of the most memorable performances I'd seen.

I didn't know he was shooting up until weeks later, and I was sad to hear it from Jono who told me he found needles in his bedroom. I mean I'd thought it was more art and less drugs.

▲

from ihatemusic.com

Re: Why Do You Listen To Noise?

I am getting more and more interested in noise. I think it's the brutality. The mind is forced silent and the purity of noise fills my head. No other music can do this, I don't care how loud it is. Sometimes I need that.

Whether it's anger, sadness, whatever emotion your feeling noise music wil help. I've realized that too.

Favorites:
Prurient
Kevin Drumm
Merzbow
John Wiese

▲

One of the most persistent lies is that boys are angry

And the shadow lie: that girls aren't angry

But even though we aren't formally trained to hate
like boys are, every girl is a natural expert:

We have so much to hate

Listen:
A growl that tastes like blood

Black reservoir
Of anger splashing
Closer than you think
Beneath the slimy dock of everything I say
In my person voice
Nice woman voice

▲

To google yellow wallpaper and find

Yellow wallpaper

I mean like swatches of it

▲

"Hysteria," writes Morris, was "a convenient diagnostic box for imprisoning women whom male doctors were unable to cure."

Today, doctors' insistence on the mysterious, unknowable nature of fibromyalgia functions as a similarly misogynistic tactic, trapping female patients in a state of uncertainty where it's impossible to assert themselves or be heard as an authority on their own experience.

Because of this notorious ambiguity, fibromyalgia is often misunderstood as nothing more than a one-size-fits-all diagnosis invented to pacify female patients with no visible symptoms—and indeed, it is sometimes misused this way. Even musician Kathleen Hanna, who was ultimately diagnosed with Lyme disease and who actively promotes awareness of invisible illness, has described fibromyalgia in this context:

"I had a doctor who dumped me in the fibromyalgia category and I just got up and left. I was just like, fuck you, I don't have fibromyalgia. That's just, to me, from what I've learned, it's a medical diagnosis dumping ground for women. They just *dump* you in there when they don't know what you have."

▲

There's another similarity between the two diagnoses: While hysteria is perhaps better remembered for dramatic symptoms like tics and convulsions, chronic pain was also a defining characteristic. In his 1859 *Treatise on Hysteria*, physician Paul Briquet observed that "pain in the muscles is so common that there is not a single woman with this neurosis who does not have some muscle pain over the course of the illness."

▲

And a third: In an 1896 report called *The Aetiology of Hysteria*, Freud concluded, "at the bottom of every case of hysteria there are one or more occurrences of premature sexual experience." As Judith Herman explains in *Trauma and Recovery*, he recognized the bizarre symptoms of hysteria as "disguised communications about sexual abuse in childhood."

Compare this to Liptan's observation that "a strong association has been shown between childhood trauma or abuse and the later development of fibromyalgia." In *Figuring Out Fibromyalgia*, she notes that "studies estimate that more than half of women with fibromyalgia have experienced childhood sexual abuse."

▲

Maybe the problem is that our only word for hysteria is: hysteria.

When the source of a woman's pain could not be located, 19th century doctors concluded that the pain was "only hysterical." Eventually, "hysteria" came to imply imagined or invented illness.

Today, in the absence of visible symptoms or clear etiology, some doctors dismiss fibromyalgia in a similar way. Patients may be sent home with prescriptions for antidepressants and hardly any acknowledgement of their physical pain. A Medscape user writes, "Physicians have told me that it is all in my head… in a degrading fashion."

Understandably, this treatment leads fibromyalgia patients to feel frustrated and angry. Another Medscape user adds, "The time has come for physicians to recognize [fibromyalgia] apart from the psychosomatic garbage that has been propagated."

And that's another side of the problem: It's not just ignorant doctors and invisible-illness skeptics who object to the validity of psychosomatic pain; this sentiment is shared by a substantial segment of people who live with chronic pain.

Our culture is quick to dismiss the emotional as illegitimate, insubstantial, not worth considering, and nobody wants their pain to be dismissed. But by refusing the connection between mind and body, we neglect an important area of research and also accept the misogynistic and foolish tradition of regarding a subset of "female" pain as nonexistent, exaggerated, imaginary, a sign of weakness.

▲

"Psychology traditionally approaches trauma through its effects on the mind. This is at best only half the story and a wholly inadequate one. Without the body and mind accessed together as a unit, we will not be able to deeply understand or heal trauma."

Peter Levine, *Waking the Tiger*

In his most recent book, *In an Unspoken Voice*, Levine observes that those who have experienced trauma often suffer from "various somatic and health complaints" with symptoms including "gastrointestinal problems, migraines, some forms of asthma, persistent pain," and more.

▲

I went to a reading last summer, and the only thing I remember about it is that one of the poets mentioned that Kenneth Patchen suffered from chronic back pain. That was the only thing I wrote down.

Google corrects "Kenneth Patchen pain" to "Kenneth Patchen paintings."

The University of Houston's library website confirms that "Kenneth Patchen's work was produced amidst constant physical pain." That passive voice. That "amidst." I see a field of pain blowing in the breeze, and Kenneth Patchen sitting in the middle of it with a notebook.

"There is body; there is mind: they are mixed up together. Shakespeare with a hole in his sock will not write the sonnet of a Shakespeare with socks intact."

Kenneth Patchen, *The Journal of Albion Moonlight*

▲

What happens when something with no name is given
a name for the first time?

What if it's the wrong name?

▲

The Spoon Theory is an absolute treasure.
The Spoon Theory is now loved by thousands of people
worldwide.
The Spoon Theory is so, so important in understanding
my life. Please, PLEASE read.

I hate the Spoon Theory.

I hate the Spoon Theory because we love it so much.
I hate the Spoon Theory because we settled for it.
I hate the Spoon Theory because we deserve better.

The Spoon Theory was invented spontaneously by a
young woman with lupus. She was at a diner with a
friend, who asked her what it was like to have the ill-
ness. In response, she gathered a dozen spoons and
handed them to the friend, explaining that the spoons
represented the finite amount of energy that she has
each day. She asked her friend to describe her daily
routine, and took away spoons as she did various tasks:
one for taking a shower, one for getting dressed, etc.
Finally the friend was left with only six spoons, and
she hadn't even made it to work yet.

The Spoon Theory is a terribly awkward metaphor for
a simple concept. Why spoons? Why 12 spoons? The
theory is not just arbitrary and imprecise, but also
problematically homespun and domestic: a wooden
spoon, a cozy kitchen, a woman's place is.

That is to say, the Spoon Theory does little to alter certain peoples' misogynist misperceptions of fibromyalgia as a fake disease invented by middle-aged women because they're lazy.

On message boards, women living with fibromyalgia, lupus, and other invisible illnesses affectionately call each other "spoonies." This cuddly vernacular matches other language we use to talk about fibromyalgia. An episode of extreme pain or fatigue is called a "flare-up." The cognition deficits experienced by some patients are called "fibro fog." Why this insistent cute-ing of illness?

As much as I abhor the patriarchal structure of western medicine, it's necessary to acknowledge that fibromyalgia patients are going to have an easier time being taken seriously by the system if they choose to code switch and talk about their illness in precise, clinical terms. It wasn't so long ago that the *Times* published "Drug Approved. Is Disease Real?" and there are still plenty of doctors who think the answer is no. Talking about the illness in terms of spoons and fog is not helping.

The reason that I can't truly hate the Spoon Theory is that it's the only way we have to express the debilitating effects of invisible illness.

I complain that it's a clumsy metaphor, but could I do better?

▲

It's possible no metaphor is adequate. In *Illness as Metaphor*, Susan Sontag observes that the use of metaphors to describe illness inevitably leads to a moralistic or punitive orientation that blames the patient for being sick. She writes: "The most truthful way of regarding illness—and the healthiest way of being ill—is one most purified of, most resistant to, metaphoric thinking."

I am proud to talk about my pain in plain language. I use similes when I find them effective—"I feel like I've been hit by a truck," etc. But mostly I just say how I feel: "I slept really badly last night and now my whole body hurts."

Once I started telling my friends about my pain, I was shocked by how immediately they were able to understand. I remember walking into Farley's to meet Carrie and saying, "I slept so badly last night," and without hesitation she said, "You must be in a lot of pain." Maybe this shouldn't have been surprising, but I was so moved by her empathy. It had seemed so impossible for anyone to understand how I felt. But all I had to do was tell them. And then they knew.

▲

But today walking thru SOMA feeling burnt out by work woke up sore my only solace the space heater which I set to "on" when I got up to feed the cat at 6:30 and thinking should I go to the reading or skip it I don't have many spoons.

Despite its inferiority, the metaphor has already burrowed into my language.

▲

I want to follow Sontag's recommendation and reject metaphor, but my illness betrays me.

Slipping the spoons back in the drawer is easy—it's the more personal metaphors that I get tangled in.

The pain started right after I recalled the rape. No coincidence. Where is Sontag on psychosomatic illness? Any psychosomatic illness, including mine, is essentially and inextricably a metaphor.

▲

When I ask myself to describe my pain, the first thing that comes to mind is this: "Woke up stiff like a coyote with rheumatism."

It's a fragment from a Richard Brautigan story that I haven't read in a long time. Strange that that's where my mind goes. But it makes sense: Stiff joints in the morning and the desperate feral identity of a coyote.

▲

Richard Brautigan was my favorite writer when I was a teenager.

I reread some of his books this year and was sad to notice a steady but subtle misogyny that I hadn't picked up when I was in high school. I missed it because it's such a gentle misogyny, gentle like everything else about Brautigan's writing.

But this line, about the coyote, is from a short story about a man who's angry at a woman because she wouldn't sleep with him after he gave her a ride home from a party. His anger takes a humorous form: It takes the shape of the puke she puked on the fender of his car, dried because he refuses to wash it off.

Brautigan puts us on the guy's side: What a cold bitch, what a poor schmuck.

And when I read the story at 16, I was squarely on the guy's side. Swayed especially by the last line: "This might have been a funny story if it weren't for the fact that people need a little loving and, God, sometimes it's sad all the shit they have to go through to find some."

It's hard to argue with this appeal to sympathy. But considered in the context of the story and in the context of Brautigan's oeuvre, that "need" for "a little loving," is a gendered need—when Brautigan says "people," he means "men." And while this sentiment passes for harmless in the story, the same sense of entitlement to female sexuality is at the root of many violent hate crimes.

Brautigan's style of misogyny—call it gentle misogyny, or subtle misogyny, or microaggressive misogyny—is woven deep throughout the fabric of our culture. Tight little stitches you can barely see. Woven so deep you could even love one of his stories so much that a phrase from it is the first thing you think of when you describe your pain—pain caused by a quiet act of violence permitted by this pervasive misogyny.

▲

Suddenly the air conditioning cuts out
And in its absence I hear a familiar growl

The growl I do when I'm feeling comfortable
Enough to feel alive

I know I have a terrible power
I identify with the ocean
i.e., I could kill people just by being myself

My growl recedes as if pulled by a tide
I smile

▲

I would like to be flogged
For every time
I end a sentence with a rising tone
You know like this?

▲

The police asked if I was lying

The police said he was a good boy

The police said I was making it up

The police asked me why I was alone there

The police kept yelling at me

The police denied my request for a female detective, which I later found out was violating procedure

The police did nothing

This cruel abuse of power is sickeningly common, and yet there's this part of me that wishes my own rape had at least had a chance at something that might pass for justice.

But when a ghost rapes you, there's no event to report. No one to report it to. It's up to you to perform your own cruel interrogation.

I asked myself if I was lying

I told myself I was making it up

I asked myself why were we alone in the exam room

I asked myself why were we alone in the exam room

I told myself maybe what he did really was normal, and maybe I'm a pervert for remembering it wrong

I kept yelling at myself

I did nothing

▲

Less than a year after he published *The Aetiology of Hysteria*, Freud repudiated his findings. He was too disturbed by their radical suggestion: If every case of hysteria was linked to abuse, then untold numbers of respectable bourgeois men in Vienna were implicated as sexual predators.

To resolve this cognitive dissonance, Freud revised his theory to say that hysteria patients were fabricating their memories of abuse.

▲

Ann Arbor never felt like a safe place
There was a professor in our department
Who thought he was Ernest Hemingway
He famously touched students' breasts
He had these signature moves
Like these tried and true tricks
For how to surreptitiously touch his students' tits
For example, The Scarf Move:
Compliment a student's scarf
At a department luncheon, then adjust it for her
So your hands each brush a nipple

And he taught there, tenure track
And everybody knew
But nobody did anything about it
His sexual harassment
Was so well-established and unquestioned
That it was like a favorite school tradition
Comfortable, cozy, cider & donuts

And every day I woke up in that town
And knew that he was touching girls
Who didn't want to be touched
It tore a hole in me
I talked about it and nobody cared
I talked about it and nothing changed
I talked about it and Rebecca said Are You Okay?
And I said yes
But what I should have said was

That's the wrong fucking question, Rebecca
What the fuck is wrong with everyone else
And why is this man still working at our school
And behaving like a monster?

▲

We watched the show as a group, in my friend's studio apartment on State Street. Mostly women, but not planned that way. We would borrow a projector from the university library, tack a sheet up on the wall, and bake a pie. *Twin Peaks* Tuesdays.

▲

What if a whole town's darkness was distilled into one man? On *Twin Peaks*, BOB has long silver hair and a maniacal laugh. He is a demonic entity clad in denim who possesses humans and leads them to commit acts of violence. Before one character commits a brutal rape and murder, he looks in the mirror and sees BOB's face instead of his own.

A circle of men stand in a forest, trying to solve a murder. Is there really an evil demon possessing people in their town?

I've heard some strange things, but this is way off the map. I'm having a hard time… believing.

Is it easier to believe a man would rape and murder his own daughter? Is it any more comforting?

Maybe that's all BOB is. The evil that men do. Maybe it doesn't matter what we call it.

▲

I've heard people say that blaming BOB for other characters' acts of violence is problematic. That it strips these characters of their guilt and enforces the misconception that men who rape and harm are all sick monsters, which ignores the social roots of violence.

Which is funny, because I always had an opposite idea of it: I thought BOB, an ugly monster who could possess any man and cause him to rape and kill, was actually the perfect metaphor for rape culture. The ongoing cycle of sexual violence. "The evil that men do."

Maybe I liked *Twin Peaks* because at least they had a team on the case, the Bookhouse Boys. Cooper, Truman, Ed, Hawk. At least somebody cared. At least somebody saw that there was a problem.

▲

Twin Peaks Tuesdays got us talking about our rapes. Erin walked me home after one of the screenings and told me about hers: In the bathroom of a frat at an Ivy League college, age 18. I told her about mine.

This was the year I learned there's a unique kind of closeness you feel with someone after you compare your experiences of sexual violence.

▲

I have this idea for a series of paintings. Which is unusual for me because I don't really paint.

The idea came to me when I was floating in a lake. I was visiting a friend I hadn't seen in a long time. We were both lying on inflatable rafts that we chose from a big pile of rafts stacked by the back door to her parents' lake house. I wanted a raft with a bottom and she found me a raft with a bottom. What I'm trying to say is that there was a feeling of abundance. Our needs were provided for. The water was warmer than I thought it would be. The lake was completely still. It was the early evening and no boats were passing by.

My friend was there to work on her screenplay.

We could have been talking about her screenplay. We could have been talking about my manuscript. We could have been talking about her sculptures. We could have been talking about my publishing project. We could have been talking about the tacos we were making for dinner, the relationships we were navigating. We could have been talking about anything.

But we were talking about rape.

Here is a painting: Two women float on rafts, bird's-eye view. You can see two stripes of a red bikini and two stripes of a blue bikini. On the shore, a dog buries its ball in the sand. The sun is just starting to set and the water is a soft greenish-black.

The title of the painting is: *Brilliant Women Talking About Rape Again (Instead of Talking About Their Art or Any Other Topic)*.

Now let me be clear: I find tremendous value in talking about rape and sharing stories of your rape with other survivors. There is great power in this, and it is necessary.

But there's this frustration I feel when I'm sitting with a brilliant and talented friend and I realize that for the past 20 or 30 minutes, we've just been talking about rape: our rapes, rape in general, rapists, rape culture, date rape, rape statistics, TV rape, rape apologists, rape flashbacks, celebrity rapists, our rapists.

In these moments, my anger vibrates inside me until it shakes loose and gains buoyancy. It floats up into the air, where it hovers directly above me and my friend and our conversation. There, it does a study for another painting called *Brilliant Women Talking About Rape Again*.

This talking is important work. Part of the violence of sexual abuse is the silence that surrounds it. How often survivors feel too much shame or guilt or trauma to speak about what happened. How this silence gives the rapes and the rapists more power.

Here is a painting: Two women sit at a kitchen table, bird's-eye view. Between them is a nearly empty cheese plate. The table is crowded with empty beer bottles and mugs stained with red wine.

Sometimes a conversation about your rape is the first conversation you have with somebody.

It was 1 a.m. or a little bit after. There had been a reading at my house, and all the other guests had left hours ago. She and I were picking at the last of the cheese plate and talking about rape.

I had met this poet before, at readings and parties, but this was the first time I'd really had a chance to talk to her. There was so much I wanted to ask her—about her childhood in Texas, the epigraph of her chapbook, her mobile library project—but I swallowed these questions. Another topic had asserted itself and it was impossible to deny.

And so I learned the facts of her life as they related to her rape: for example, that she went to college in Austin, but moved away when she was 23 ("the whole time I lived in Austin I was afraid of running into him").

Here is a painting: Two women talk in a bookstore, bird's-eye view. One sits in a pale blue armchair, and one browses the shelves. The books are disorganized, but in a welcoming way. Other customers come and go.

We could have been talking about her literary magazine, or the talk she was planning for the Berkeley ecopoetics conference. But.

Here is a painting: Two women sit at a bar, bird's-eye view. Each one has a beer in front of her. TVs mounted high in two corners of the room show sports highlights.

We could have been talking about our lyric essays, her letterpress studio. But.

There was so much I wanted to ask this poet. I had heard her read an essay a few months before that so gracefully accomplished everything my own essays aim to do in regards to writing the body into the text and making the personal universal.

Maybe it was because I was shy; I didn't know how to just blurt out, "Tell me how you wrote your stunning essay." Or I tried and it was a hard conversation to start. Anyway, the topic didn't really pick up and we found ourselves talking about rape instead.

"I don't know anyone who hasn't been raped," the poet said. "It's like that Claudia Rankine quote."

She lent me her copy of Rankine's *Don't Let Me Be Lonely*, and I flipped through it on the train ride home. There it was, on page 72: "I think surely some percentage of women hasn't been raped. I don't know though, really. Perhaps this is the kind of thing I could find out on Google."

In order to reconcile the ubiquity of rape, we need more images of rape as it actually looks—i.e., it's rarely a violent struggle with a stranger followed by a helpful trip to the police department.

And in order to understand the impact of rape, we need more images of how rape stays with us—i.e., it's not just something that happens one night.

That's what these paintings are about. They are visualizing how much of a woman's life can be spent processing the trauma of sexual violence, helping other women heal, strategizing ways to make safer communities. They are honoring the work we are doing in these conversations.

I think of the subversive WPA murals, grand cubist factory scenes with a little hammer and sickle in the corner. These paintings have the same motivation: to celebrate the strength of the worker while also criticizing the system that forces her to work.

I would very much like to walk into a room full of these paintings.

So then why won't I paint them?

It's not that I don't have any paint. And it's not that I'm an awful painter. And it's not that I don't have the time.

It's that someone else should paint them.

I don't want these paintings to be paintings of me and my friends having these conversations. I think a lot of us are having these conversations. If not in lakes, in oceans. If not in bars, in cafes. These paintings are of all of us. These paintings are yours to paint.

▲

Last summer I went to a church bazaar sale and found a blue and white spiral-bound notebook labeled The Scholastic Book Club's Millennium Time Capsule Contest. Here was an invitation to time travel. I bought it for 50 cents.

This kind of moving through time is something every survivor of trauma is an expert at. I was determined to win the contest. I signed the pledge on the cover: "I do hereby agree to record my experiences, thoughts, and feelings in this diary during the millennial year 2000. Furthermore, I agree that I will seal this diary in an envelope on December 31, 2000, and I will not open this envelope until January 1, 2010."

My unique time-travel approach would give me an edge and set me apart from the other contestants. I filled the journal nearly halfway, combining current reflections with memories from 2000.

After a few months of writing, I lost interest in the Time Capsule notebook. When I took a closer look at the cover, I realized it wasn't an entry into the contest, but a prize for those who had already won. I realized the writing I was doing in it wasn't any different from the writing I do in other notebooks; my writing often corresponds between past and present. And the fat spiral binding and small pages hurt my hand.

Even on regular paper, writing makes my hand cramp up like a claw. The pain reminds me of a bronze sculpture I saw on Lauren Berlant's Facebook page of an arm that's on one end an open hand and on the other, a clenched fist.

"A relation of cruel optimism exists when something you desire is actually an obstacle to your flourishing."

Lauren Berlant

No notebook reverie goes unpunished. It's always a question of: What's worth writing down?

▲

In the workshop we are asked to add a noise
To our motion
I am shy around my own noise
So I breathe
Loud
And the breath becomes a growl
I am not surprised

I am embarrassed by my growl
Though it's exactly what I'm here to do
I am getting, would be getting
An A-plus in the workshop
If I growled out loud

I mean not an A-plus
But Bhanu would give me a talisman
And offer to blurb my book
That kind of thing
Just kidding

Women don't want literary fame

▲

A couple of weeks ago, I found out that a man I used to date raped someone I know. The next morning, I woke up from a dream about him. The morning after that, I woke up crying. Hearing about this rape reminded me of my own rape, and it reminded a lot of my friends about their own rapes, too.

In *King Kong Theory*, Virginie Despentes asks, "How shall we explain the fact that you hardly ever hear the other side of the story, 'I raped so and so, on this day, in these circumstances'?"

▲

We don't want to believe our friends are rapists. But this popular desire to hold onto the comforting *SVU* falsehood that a rapist is a stranger in a shadowy alleyway—and only a stranger in a shadowy alleyway—is causing us a lot of trouble.

After Dylan Farrow wrote an open letter accusing her stepfather of childhood sexual abuse, my Facebook feed was flooded with articles about the controversy. One thing I read that I liked was an article called "Woody Allen Is Not a Monster: He Is a Person. Like My Father."

The author writes: "That this darkness is actually woven into and throughout the fabric of our society—that these abusers are among us—is simply too much to bear. So the darkness is ignored except for the most distilled, theatrical, and viscerally repellent cases."

▲

After learning about the recent rape, I find myself in a hyper-vigilant state. I don't feel safe. My boyfriend assures me that I'm safe, but what he doesn't understand is that there's this other kind of knowing that you're safe that's far away from logic or present reality.

I am not being raped, have not been raped in 20 years, will hopefully not ever be raped again, but I am also continuously being raped. The trauma has lodged in my brain and in my body.

I am so used to the pain. It's part of me. It feels like just another body part. An always-clenching in my shoulders, neck, back, legs, hands.

▲

I'm 31 but I feel like I'm 60. People in my life may think I am exaggerating but I am always in pain. Every morning I wake up feeling like I was run over by a truck. I feel like I've been hit by a bus. I wake up stiff like a coyote with rheumatism. I wake up in the woods on a bed of dried moss. I have a doctor I have a wolf I have an ex. Interrupting me, stepping out from behind the same tree to block my path. Invisible, impossible to prove. Whether or not you believe me. Imagine it repeating like a GIF.

▲

It's only when the pain is severe or when the pain prevents me from doing something that I'm forced to think about it. But even when I'm not thinking about it, it's still there.

My body is washing dishes and it's in pain. My body is on hold with California Blue Cross Blue Shield and it's in pain. My body is dancing and it's in pain. My body is Skyping Beth and it's in pain. My body is taking a shower and it's in pain. My body is riding BART and it's in pain. My body is politely saying no and it's in pain. My body is reading a book and it's in pain. My body is at work and it's in pain. My body is writing this and it's in pain. My body is walking to meet you and it's in pain.

Afterword

When I started writing *Tender Points* in 2013, my experience of pain was a lonely one. Friends and partners did their best to understand, but I didn't know anyone else living with chronic pain. I was isolated from other chronically ill people and survivors of assault, so my pain and my assault felt like personal problems I needed to sort out. That's why I started writing the book.

What I didn't know when I started writing—what I didn't know I could even hope for—was that the process of researching, writing, and reading from *Tender Points* would eventually connect me to other sick people and survivors and introduce me to sick and disabled communities.

In researching my book, I encountered voices that made me feel less alone. Carolyn Lazard's essay "How to Be a Person in the Age of Autoimmunity" was the first time I saw a writer draw connections between chronic illness and capitalism, and the first time I saw a writer describe doctors' failures to understand or treat their illness. In Sini Anderson's documentary *The Punk Singer,* I encountered Kathleen Hanna's anger and vulnerability around Lyme disease as well as footage of her haunting early-career performance piece about childhood sexual abuse.

I remember reading from my manuscript at the Long Haul in Berkeley. After the reading, an audience member asked if they could give me a hug. "I've never met anyone else with fibromyalgia before," they explained. And then I realized: neither had I. Writing a book about fibromyalgia had led me to making a friend with fibromyalgia. I was starting to feel less alone in my pain.

When *Tender Points* was first published in 2015 (by the well-loved and now-defunct Timeless, Infinite Light), I went on a weeklong East Coast tour with fellow Timeless author Paul Ebenkamp. During this tour I had the chance to read with Carolyn and others at Bluestockings in New York and read with Tyler Vile in Baltimore and DC. I hadn't met Tyler before, but I immediately felt a connection with her. Her first book, *Never Coming Home*, had just come out from Topside and, like *Tender Points,* it deals with themes of disability and sexual abuse. It felt good to share a stage with her—and it felt good to share the project of talking about these difficult subjects.

Participating in interviews about the book was another way I connected with people. I remember meeting up with my friend Feliks Garcia in New York so he could interview me about trauma and memory for his podcast. Sadly, Feliks passed away a few months after that meeting. I never got to listen to our interview but I have no doubt it's one of the most vulnerable conversations I've ever had about my abuse because Feliks was so gentle, thoughtful, and easy to talk to.

In 2016, with Catherine Fryszczyn, Carolyn, Johanna Hedva, Emji Saint Spero, and others, I co-organized Sick Fest, a free and accessible day of performances by sick and disabled artists in Oakland. Sick Fest introduced me to a wide range of performers and also to the groups they belonged to. It was in reading performers' bios that I learned about the renowned Bay Area-based disability performance project Sins Invalid. And it was through Sins Invalid that I learned about disability justice.

Later that year, Catherine bought me a ticket to a Sins Invalid show called *Birthing, Dying, Becoming Crip Wisdom*. Early in the evening, Leah Lakshmi Piepzna-Samarasinha performed "Crip Fairy Godmother," a poem in which she warns a newly disabled addressee about the isolation and invisibility they'll likely experience— but also promises them that something better awaits: a warm, wise, interdependent community ready to welcome them into the fold. Her poem felt like a spell. By believing it, by living it, I could make it true.

Over the next couple of years, I joined a chronic illness listserv, a Facebook group for Sick & Disabled Queers, and another online group for disabled writers. I made friends with Sini and talked to her about chronic illness and artmaking. I interviewed her about *So Sick*, her in-progress documentary on the late-stage Lyme epidemic, and published our conversation in *Bitch*. Not long after, I got to know Maya Dusenbery, the author of *Doing Harm: The Truth About How Bad Medicine and Lazy Science Leave Women Dismissed, Misdiagnosed, and Sick.* I met Maya because she was collecting bad "doctor stories" for her book. Later, when she visited the Bay Area, I had the pleasure of writing a profile of her for *Wolfman New Life Quarterly.* Currently, I'm in correspondence with Caren Beilin about her forthcoming book, *Blackfishing the IUD*, which exposes the serious and lasting side effects of the copper IUD.

A bad doctor story is never a story of one bad doctor—it's a story of an inherently flawed and biased system, a story about discrimination and power. There is no shortage of bad doctor stories, and this is a good thing. We need all the illness and disability narratives we can get. We are lucky to be living in what truly seems to be a renaissance of art and activism about chronic illness and disability.

Likewise, it's been inspiring to witness the recent explosion of conversation about rape and abuse. We need these narratives, too. As with bad doctor stories, each story of sexual violence isn't just about a single incident—it's about the culture and power dynamics that allow for this to happen and keep happening. Bad doctor stories and stories of sexual violence are so important. They spread necessary information and make others know they're not alone. And I believe they can lead to change.

I'm still in pain. I still feel exhausted every morning, no matter how many hours I've slept. But I don't feel alone in my pain anymore. I feel like I'm in conversation, I feel like I'm in community. I'm grateful to the individuals, groups, books, performances, songs, podcasts, protests, Instagram posts, documentaries, art projects, and articles that remind me I'm not alone in my pain, that I'm part of something bigger. Some people have told me that *Tender Points* helped them feel less alone. I very much hope it can continue to do that.

in solidarity,
Amy Berkowitz

San Francisco
July 2019

Acknowledgements

Thank you to Ashley Brim, Matt Carney, Tom Comitta, Carrie Hunter, Alena Kastin, Carolyn Lazard, Tzuriel Monk, Nico Peck, Marissa Petrou, Yosefa Raz, Thurston, Zoe Tuck, Laura Woltag, and Stephanie Young for your edits and support and friendship.

Thank you to Simon Crafts and Jordan Gower and everybody at Alley Cat for making a welcoming space to write.

Thank you to the people whose message board comments I've collaged in this book, and to everyone who participates in online communities to make the experience of illness less alienating.

Excerpts of this text were previously published in *580 Split, Drunken Boat, LOVEbook, Sparkle + Blink, Uprooted,* and *VIDA: Women in Literary Arts*. Thank you to Garin Hay, Lindsey Boldt, Amanda Huckins, Evan Karp, Megan Winkelman, and Emily Brandt.

Thank you to Joel Gregory and Emji Saint Spero at Timeless for your belief in this project from the beginning. Thank you to Stephen Motika, Lindsey Boldt, Kazim Ali, and Andrea Abi-Karam at Nightboat for giving it a second life.

Works consulted

"A Thing About Rats." *Teenage Mutant Ninja Turtles*.
Dir. Yoshikatsu Kasai.

"Arbitrary Law." *Twin Peaks*. Dir. David Lynch.

Brautigan, Richard. *Revenge of the Lawn*.

Berlant, Lauren. *Cruel Optimism*.

Briquet, Paul. *Treatise on Hysteria*.

Buzzeo, Melissa. Vital Forms: Healing and the Arts of
Crisis. Berkeley, CA. 2013.

Carson, Anne. *Glass, Irony and God*.

Crofford, Leslie. "Fibromyalgia." *American College of
Rheumatology*.

Despentes, Virginie. *King Kong Theory*.

Di Prima, Diane. *Revolutionary Letters*.

"Except for That One Thing." *This American Life*.
Narr. Ira Glass.

Freud, Sigmund. *The Aetiology of Hysteria*.

Herman, Judith. *Trauma and Recovery*.

Hoffman, Diane E., and Anita J. Tarzian. "The Girl Who Cried
Pain: A Bias Against Women in the Treatment of Pain."

hooks, bell. *The Will to Change: Men, Masculinity, and Love.*

Kelley, Mike. *Horizontal Tracking Shot of a Cross Section of Trauma Rooms.*

Kuppers, Petra. "Futures of Contact Improvisation." *Contact Quarterly.*

Levine, Peter. *In an Unspoken Voice.*

Levine, Peter. *Waking the Tiger.*

Liptan, Ginevra. *Figuring Out Fibromyalgia.*

Marcus, Sara. *Girls to the Front.*

Miller, Jenni. "'Punk Singer' Kathleen Hanna on Riot Grrrls Grown Up." *Film.com.*

Miserandino, Christine. "The Spoon Theory." *But You Don't Look Sick.*

Morris, David B. *The Culture of Pain.*

National Institute of Health. "Questions and Answers About Fibromyalgia." *National Institute of Health.*

National Vulvodynia Association. "HBO's 'Sex and the City' Portrays a Serious Women's Health Condition With Inaccuracy." *National Vulvodynia Association.*

Patchen, Kenneth. *The Journal of Albion Moonlight*.

The Punk Singer. Dir. Sini Anderson.

Rankine, Claudia. *Don't Let Me Be Lonely*.

"The Real Me." *Sex and the City*. Dir. Michael Patrick King.

Scarry, Elaine. *The Body in Pain*.

Socialist Patients' Collective. *Turn Illness into a Weapon*.

Sontag, Susan. *Illness As Metaphor*.

Stetka, Bret. "What Is Fibromyalgia? Medscape Readers Weigh In." *Medscape*.

Strain, Donovan. "I Found Ice Cube's Good Day." *Murk Avenue*.

Warwick, William. "Woody Allen Is Not a Monster: He Is a Person. Like My Father." *Gawker*.

Winchester Mystery House. "Sarah Winchester, Woman of Mystery." *Winchester Mystery House*.

Wojnarowicz, David. *Close to the Knives*.

Nightboat Books

Nightboat Books, a nonprofit organization, seeks to develop audiences for writers whose work resists convention and transcends boundaries. We publish books rich with poignancy, intelligence, and risk. Please visit nightboat.org to learn about our titles and how you can support our future publications.

The following individuals have supported the publication of this book. We thank them for their generosity and commitment to the mission of Nightboat Books:

Kazim Ali
Anonymous
Jean C. Ballantyne
Photios Giovanis
Amanda Greenberger
Elizabeth Motika
Benjamin Taylor
Peter Waldor
Jerrie Whitfield & Richard Motika

Nightboat Books gratefully acknowledges support from the Topanga Fund, which is dedicated to promoting the arts and literature of California.